How to Boost Your Credit Score in 30 Days

Fast Credit Score

0 - 850

AUTHOR NAME:

Art McCoy

CONTENTS

LEGAL NOTES

DISCLAIMER AND/OR LEGAL NOTICES:

INTRODUCTION

In this book, I'm going to show you how to boost your credit score fast. So if you want a better credit, reading this entire book will be the cheapest investment you can make on yourself and on your credit score. And why should you care? Well, remember if you will have the best credit score, especially if you pick up just one or two tricks in this book, out of the many tricks that I offer here, you'll get better interest rates on your loans on the first place, and you'll actually get loans, which you can use loans to make money. And if you have a cheaper interest rate, you'll save money.

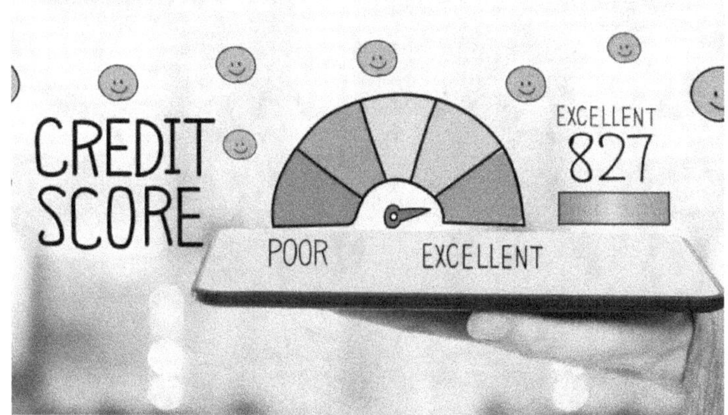

PART 1: SHORT TERM PLANS (1)

CHAPTER 1. CREDIT ALGORITHM

This is probably the most important thing to try to imagine, because when you think like the credit algorithm does, you'll be able to boost your credit score much easier.

So here's the thing. When you think about the credit algorithm, think about basically a God. Let's call him, credit God. Here's what we know about this God. He tends to check in on you every 14 to 30 days. And once to see if you're up to the same habits that you've been up to in the past, or did something change, the keyword is changed because when something changes, that's when the credit God makes an adjustment to your credit score.

GOOD CHANGE, YOU GO UP. BAD CHANGE, YOU GO DOWN.

The credit God tends to raise his eyebrows at kind of things that we ordinarily wouldn't think that he would. And that's a lot of what this book is about. So I'm going to show you some tricks to put to use, to get you into the God's graces, a fast credit God's graces.

Now, you've probably seen this before, but let's just call this a quick recap of the kind of the credit that God looks for. The credit God is checking on you with the following priority: 35% of the credit God's opinion is based on your timely payments. Basically, when you pay your bills on time and God may raise his eyebrow at the pattern in which you pay your bills. I'll talk about those tricks in a moment.

BEING 30 DAYS LATE

Being 30 days late, just a heads up, means you were literally a full 30 days late. So if you pay a bill that's, let's say due on September 1st and you pay it as late as September 30th, technically, you're not considered 30 days late. Now, you might get a late fee from your lender because maybe your bill was due on the first and late on the 15th.

You might have to pay a fee, but you actually have to be a full 30 days late for something to affect your credit. Now don't do this. You don't want to pay late fees. And if the credit God sees that you're paying late fees, he might raise his eyebrows as well. But there's really nothing worse than being late on your payments, especially if your 30 day late turned into 60 or 90 days late. Those are obviously worse than 30 days late. Also the more recent the late is, the more of an impact that will have. So, 35% of your credit score tends to be based on your payment history.

CREDIT UTILIZATION

The second thing the credit God looks at, is how much of our available debt we're using. This is called credit utilization. The credit God generally wants to see that if we have $1000 dollars of credit available, we're using no more than $300 of it. Otherwise, the credit God tends to think that we're in distress. And that goes for individual accounts and our total credit. Both of these should be under 30%. We'll talk tricks for this in just a moment.

TYPES OF CREDIT:

Credit God is going to look at how good you are at juggling multiple different kinds of credit, which I've got some great tricks for this coming up.

Having a variety is a very good idea, especially if you're trying to boost your score to get into owning real estate sooner rather than later. Then the credit God's going to look and to see how much of your credit portfolio is new. If you've all of a sudden gotten a ton of new credit, that could be a little bit of a red flag to the credit God. It seems that for some reason, you need a bunch more money. However, this is only going to be about a 10% to 12% factor of your credit score because sometimes there are people who make their payments on time and they have a very low utilization, but they would like having a bunch of different rewards cards or different lines of credit. So, this is going to be about a 10% to 12% impact.

LENGTH OF YOUR CREDIT HISTORY

Then the length of your credit history applies as well, but that is only at about 5% to 7%. It is much less important, because again, you can have a short but good history, which is a lot better than a bad but long history. So 65% of your score comes from just two things: Paying on time and using less than 30% of what you have available.

CHAPTER 2. CREDIT REPORT

Now, let's talk about some short-term changes that we can make. Part one of short-term changes, starts with knowing what we're dealing with.

I personally recommended going to annualcreditreport.com. This is the official, triple credit reporting website that will show you all of your three scores. And this is the one, the federal government sanctions to say everybody's entitled to their credit report, once a year, with all three bureaus. Run all three of your credit reports at once.

You're going to check all your information. Make sure there are no incorrect mailing addresses and your social security number is correct. Make sure that your former employers are correct and any other indicators that can identify you versus potentially identity thieves. It is very important to make sure that all of this information is correct. So if there's any incorrect information, make sure you dispute it. The sooner you do, the better.

Then, you want to go through all of the items on your credit report. You don't want to ignore something that's bad. If you don't recognize something, you got to dispute it. When in doubt, dispute it. Seriously, it's as easy as pressing a button.

THREE CREDIT BUREAUS

In fact, the next step is opening an account at each of the bureaus. You can go to TransUnion.com and sign up for a true identity plan which is completely free. I shouldn't even call it a plan. It's just a login. You sign in and you can monitor your credit directly through TransUnion. Now that's just one of the three bureaus. You should also then go to MyEquifax.com and set up a free account there. Just a heads up, all of these companies are going to try to sell you something. You do not have to pay a single dollar.

Once you set up the accounts, you'll be able to dispute any errors that you find on your credit reports with those bureaus. When you run all three of your credit reports, you'll see which reports and which companies are reporting potentially wrong information.

Again, when in doubt, dispute it. Experian.com is your stop number three. Make sure you set at an account at each of these bureaus. This is nice to have, and if you need to get on the phone with any of these bureaus, always remember, even if you hate your guts, at least pretend to be nice. The nicer you are, the easier it is, to get your disputes resolved.

Remember to tell people that you're trying to make a change to get into the credit God's Good graces. Everybody wants to be in the credit God's good graces. Usually, when other people find that you are trying to make a change, they help you. The same goes with any kind of companies that are trying to collect debt from you that you have to talk to, the nicer you are, the better. Remember, these are just employees and whatever you can do to get them in your good graces, helps you get your problems solved.

CHANGE

Now, the next thing to remember is change. If you're not happy with your score, you've got to change what you're doing. The algorithm, the credit God, looks for change. And remember this: the credit God has a memory of about seven years for most things like late payments, on time payments and collections. Chapter seven, bankruptcy liquidations, do show up for about 10 years. But don't get discouraged. The credit God is going to prioritize your recent behaviors, when determining your credit score.

You could literally have a perfect credit score, and then all of a sudden make a bunch of credit mistakes, like messing up your utilization and open a ton of new accounts and the credit God's going to look and say, Oh, maybe your situation has changed and your score can tank very quickly.

Recent changes are really big weights when it comes to your credit score. Although the actual formula is pretty secret, we've got a lot of tips and tricks coming up right now. And before we get into some of the tips and tricks, if you haven't yet gotten any kind of credit, make sure as soon as you're 18 years old apply for credit cards like Apple card or Discover it® Secured Card. Whatever you can do to get your first credit card, is going to get help you get your foot in the door and I recommend you pay it off in full every month. Don't get a credit card just to max out your limit. Ideally, keep your card paid off.

PART 2: SHORT TERM PLANS (PART 2)

CHAPTER 1. FAST CREDIT BOOST

STEP 1:

Now, let's get into some real tips and tricks that we can use in the short term. So I am going to call short-term part 2.

The first thing we can do to boost our credit is to open up secured loans or secured lines of credit. You take $200 that you have, and you open an account at a credit union, and then you go to different credit unions and do the same thing. Then, you ask the credit union to open a secured personal loan or personal line of credit, which most credit unions offer these. You could do this at two or three different banks. And because these are secured, you end up paying very little interest on them. And if you get a line of credit, sometimes you don't have to pay any interest at all. Make your payments timely. And now all of a sudden, if you have a credit card and three of these lines of credit, the credit God looks and says, wow, you went from one credit card to three lines of credit and a credit card, and you're paying them all timely. That's awesome. That is a great way to build your credit fast. It gives you that variety to your credit profile.

STEP 2:

Step number two, or option number two, to boost your credit score quickly is to see if a family member can add you onto one of his credit accounts as an authorized user. This doesn't hurt him but it can help you a lot, because it shows that you have a longer history of credit. Make sure you get onto somebody's account who has a positive history. You will inherit that positive history and you don't affect him at all. That long history gets added onto yours and helps you build your credit as a quick stepping stone. It is a great idea.

STEP 3:

The next thing you could do is ask for a credit line increase by calling your credit card companies. Generally, for loyal customers, they're more than happy to boost your credit limit. The cool thing about this is, if you have $1000 credit limit and you're using $300 of it. That means you've got about a 30% credit utilization. However, if you ask them to increase your credit limit, to say $2,000, now you're only using 15% of your available credit.

However, you want to be careful with this one. You have to know yourself. If you're going to immediately spend all that money from your new credit limit, maybe don't ask for a credit limit increase. Some people will actually ask for a credit line decrease to prevent them from being able to swipe their card and getting into more debt. So in this scenario, your personality is more important than trying to have the lowest utilization possible. Your ultimate goal is to get out of debt and stop paying credit card rates or other kinds of high interest rate debt. So if that means lowering your credit available limit, do it.

STEP 4:

Stop opening new lines of credit. This is an easy short-term change. Just stop opening new cards, stop churning credit cards for a time being, take a pause, take a breather and just don't open any new accounts. Remember, you're trying to send a signal to the credit Gods that you've changed your way, and you're not always looking for new lines of credit. Do that once your score is higher and then it'll matter less, anyway.

STEP 5:

Try to get current and do whatever you can, to make multiple payments per month. If you usually have a bill that's due, let's say September 15th, and you always wait until September 14th to pay that down. The credit God sees that you're pretty much always paying at the last minute possible. If instead, you change your habits and start paying down your balances multiple times per month and paying your minimum early and then you pay two or three more times and doing this regularly, the credit God is going to notice. He says: Wow, Okay, awesome. We've got a totally changed habit here and now we're paying early. He sees the balances are going down every time he checks in on you. And that's a really good signal. Remember, you're trying to signal to the credit God, your credit changes and behavior changes.

STEP 6:

Try to stay away from large purchases, especially in the short term when you're trying to boost your credit. So if all of a sudden, you spend like a grand on a new refrigerator and you put it on a credit card but you usually only spend like $250 a month, and now all of a sudden you're spending $1000, the credit God doesn't know that your refrigerator broke. He just looks at that and sees, Oh, you usually use $250 a credit but now you use $1000. Hmm. Okay. We're going to drop your score a little bit, because something's going on over here, possibly. He doesn't know that your refrigerator broke, anyway.

STEP 7:

Paying down collections can help, but it depends how old they are. Remember the more recent an account is, the more of an impact it will have. So sometimes paying off old obligations, like old collections that are already closed and they're getting ready to fall off that seven year snapshot look back, sometimes doesn't make much of a difference. But if you have a relatively new collection within the last two years, sometimes it's a good idea to call those credit companies, or collection companies up and see if you can either negotiate a balance or have them show your account as paid in full, even if you end up negotiating something. Remember, whatever you negotiate, be nice and get whatever you do in writing. It is very important.

STEP 8:

Avoid the balanced myth. There's a myth that you have to carry a balance to see your score go up. It's totally wrong. You do not need to carry a balance on your cards. However, you should use a card every so often to prevent that card company from closing your account for a lack of use. When you close cards or close accounts, you lose that history. So usually I recommend if you've had a card for four or five years, don't close it. Even if you stop using it, just buy a pack of gum once every six months or whatever. Pay it down. Don't forget to pay it, though. Because, you don't want to get 30 days late and be done. I personally recommend everything that could affect your social security or your credit score via your social security number, have it written down on a sheet that you check two or three times per month, that'll prevent you from being late.

STEP 9:

Avoid when possible introductory interest rates. This is mostly a psychological issue. Now there are times, you can really play this game and move around balances and make a lot of money by, or save a lot of money by moving balances around with introductory teaser rates like 0% for the first six months or whatever. But these rates are designed to eventually trap you into a higher fee loan. So be careful of that.

STEP 10:

Consider a consolidating credit company. This way, instead of paying like five to 10 different credit cards or debts, you can pay them in one account. Consider a company like SoFi Credit consolidation, , or just any of these credit consolidation loan companies. You can shop and search for one on Google. And see if you can get one big loan that has a lower interest rate. That will let you to immediately pay off five or six different bills. And now, you're only working away at chopping away that one loan. And pay that one off as soon as you can. The cool thing about those loans is when you pay that loan off every month; you can't really just swipe the card and get that balance back up like what you can do with a credit card. So sometimes, those credit consolidation loans are pretty good.

PART 3: LONG TERM PLANS

CHAPTER 1. LONG TERM CHANGES

Then, you want to get into some long term changes here. Here are the long-term changes:

STEP 1:

The first long-term change that you want to make is to consider the two week rule. The two week rule means that you're going to apply for new loans on a two week period. The credit Gods are going to assume, when they look at your portfolio and they see that you have applied for three loans in just the last two weeks. Let's say you're shopping for a home loan or whatever. The credit God doesn't actually think that you're trying to get three home loans at once; instead, the credit God will usually consolidate these inquiries and make it seem like you only really had one credit check within a two week period, because they're assuming that you're doing the right thing and you're shopping around for the best possible deal. So, if you're going to apply for new credits, trying to do it within a two week period.

STEP 2:

Stay and get below that 30% utilization per account and in total. Now, some credit bureaus only care if you're above a 35% utilization and some care if you're above 30%. So I just recommend try to get under 30%. So, you kind of hit both of those.

STEP 3:

In the long-term changes, try to separate business and personal expenses. Not only the expenses, but also the loan accounts you have. So for example, talk to a CPA or an entity attorney or a business attorney to see if you can open an S-corporation and run your side hustle through an S-corporation. Now, you can apply for loans, like car loans, credit card loans, or lines of credit through your business. And worst case scenario, if you're late on one of those, it's not going to show up on your personal credit report. Sometimes, you still have to agree that you'll personally guarantee those loans, but they usually don't show up on your personal credit report, which is really cool. That means, your good positive history doesn't show up in them either, but it also helps you keep your credit utilization low. So that way, if you need money for a new business idea or a new division to your company or a new project you're working on for your company, it's better to use your business lines of credit or your business credit cards than your personal credit cards. So, that way you keep your personal credit, nice and safe, and you keep that low utilization.

STEP 4:

Open new accounts and expand your credit variety while reducing your utilization. So, if you're using say 30% of your credit, but then you open up new accounts, you might actually be lowering your utilization just by opening up new accounts.

Now, in the short term, you don't want to open up new accounts. You want to do this in the long-term. You know, once you start getting your score up after you get that first, big, 30 day boost, maybe three, four months down the road, then you start trying to bump your credit by opening up a variety of counts. And it's really only after those three or four months that you really want to start thinking about applying for new credit cards or loans. Anyway, maybe even just wait the full six months, because realistically, once you get to that 740, 750, you might be able to qualify for that Chase Sapphire and that Chase Freedom card that a lot of folks are waiting to get to qualify for. So, you may as well use the short term boosts first and then apply for the cards using the two week rule, once you're ready. And you can monitor your credit scores growth using an app like Credit Karma.

STEP 5:

Credit Freeze. This is like way underused. Freezing your credit is totally free and doesn't affect your score from going up or down. All it does, it prevents somebody else from opening a fraudulent account, using your social security number and your date of birth.

And if somebody opens up a fraudulent account under your name, let's say on Macy's and rack up $3,000 worth of charges, you might end up getting stuck with a collection, even though your identity was stolen. A credit freeze helps prevent this and it's totally free to do it. Usually, you could even do it through the portals that you made earlier on myEquifax, TransUnion and Experian websites. Otherwise, just Google TransUnion credit freeze, Equifax credit freeze, and Experian credit freeze. It's a smart thing to do. Now, this does mean though that when you go to unfreeze your credit, you will have to unfreeze your credit and do that manually. It usually takes about 15 to 20 minutes to do, and you should make sure that you've written down your pin numbers and all the information that you need to be able to unlock your credit again. And remember your credit can still grow while your credit frozen.

Quick fun note to know is that most of banks will give you the best pricing once you get to about a 740 to 760 credit score. Beyond that, it makes no difference. So once you get to 740, 760 you've pretty much arrived. Then you can go open up accounts, just unfreeze your credit and go open accounts and use them to make money, which we're going to talk about one of my favorite ways to make money in a moment.

But remember, for most banks once you get 740 to 760, you're good. You basically get the same pricing that somebody with a score of 850 or 820 gets. It can be somewhere between 740 and 760, depending on the bank. So to be safe, say 760 plus.

STEP 6:

If you're worried about your identity and you think there's a possibility that your social security number and your date of birth was compromised, and you might be worried about identity theft, consider looking into insurances like NortonLifeLock also not sponsored. This helps reimburse you from damages that occur if your identity gets stolen. They might provide you, like a million dollar policy coverage. So that way, if your identity gets stolen, they will spend that money on attorneys and helping you get your credit back to normal and helping you pay off any kind of collections that may have appeared. They'll also help you monitor your credit. But remember, monitoring and insurance are different from freezing your credit, which just locks it out entirely.

STEP 7:

Getting into owning real estate. Real estate is a very easy and consistent way to build your credit. You set up auto pay and you make your payment early and you immediately look good in the graces of the credit God. It shows massive responsibility in handling a large loan and paying consistently and early every month. However, if you delay in paying your mortgage, the credit God starts wandering what the heck is going on.

Thank you so much for reading this book. Hopefully you learned a lot about short-term methods that you can use to boost your credit quickly within 30 days and some longer-term methods to boost your credit in the long-term.

And remember the credit God is looking for credit changes. So remember, change is good.

ABOUT THE AUTHOR

I am a licensed realtor and mortgage loan originator in Southern California. With my Real Estate and Mortgage experience dating back to the early 2000s, I continue to mold myself to become better, stronger and sharper within the mortgage industry despite the market challenges that may arise.

CAN I ASK FOR A FAVOUR?

If you enjoyed this book, found it useful or otherwise then I'd really appreciate it if you would post a short review on Amazon. I do read all the reviews personally so that I can continually write what people are wanting.